Introduction

While creating this book my plan was to motivate, inspire, and encourage you to believe in yourself by using positive thinking and positive affirmations. The definition of affirm is to show a strong belief in something or to show an abundant amount of dedication to it. When you affirm something, you can do it publically or internally. After reading this book you will have the confidence to affirm greatness over your life.

Over the last 10 years I have been coaching, teaching, and mentoring students at the middle and high school level. I've noticed a lot of students don't understand the benefits of thinking and speaking positively. Life can get challenging at times and negative thoughts can linger in our minds. My goal is to help people learn how to decrease and delete those negative thoughts.

In the litmus test and the glass half empty or half full proverbial phase individuals get a glimpse of different ways to view life. The goal in life is to change from the pessimistic glass half empty perspective, to an optimistic view of the glass is half full. Life is about perspective and the way we think about our experiences. Our thoughts can control our feelings and even determine our outcomes. If you are able to embrace and implement the ideas and strategies in this book, then you are sure to live a more satisfying life. A life that allows you to live out your true greatness. We all have been blessed with the opportunity of life and we should live our lives to the fullest. We should do things we enjoy, love, and care about. Therefore, we need not worry about what other people think of us. GOD wants us to enjoy every moment of our life. I believe the obstacles we face are opportunities for us to grow, learn, and mature. Let me ask you this, what do you think GOD wants for you? Do you think GOD wants you living a life of fear, worry, doubt, and poverty? Or does GOD want you to live a life full of joy, happiness, abundance and love? It's up to you to make the choice of living your greatest life. Just TRUST GOD, BELIVE, and have CONFIDENCE in yourself. GOD never makes mistakes. Everything in our life happens for a reason. We must know that life is great, life is always getting better, and know that we are going to accomplish our goals. Just like we know the sun rises every morning we must know GOD is with us every day.

GOD wants us to live a life full of joy, love, happiness and abundance.

Remember, YOU ARE GREAT!!!

I am a Creator and I live the life that I want

The first step to understanding that you are a Creator is believing in your own powers. God has blessed us with the ability to create the life that we want. Focus on the aspects of life that you can control and let GOD handle the rest. Focus on what you want to create for your life. Do not let challenges change your thoughts from positive to negative. You have been blessed with wonderful life and GOD wants the best for you therefore you should want the same. Repeat this affirmation throughout your day and write out everything you want to create in your life. While writing down what you want for your life trust, know, and believe everything will happen at the perfect time in your life. Be patient and look at any obstacle that you face as a learning lesson. Keep your eyes on the prize and do not focus on anything negative. When creating the life that you want you have to see the end result and imagine how you will feel when you reach your goals. Hold on to that feeling. Your task for today and this week is to write out your life goals. Do not limit yourself, therefor you should THINK BIG! You can have and do anything you put your mind to. Make a realistic plan and trust that GOD will guide you during the process of achieving your goals and living the life you want to create. Read your life plan and goals every day. At least 2 times a day. When you wake up and before you go to bed. Read it as many times as you can. The more you read and see your goals, the more you will believe them. Know, trust, and believe in yourself. Most importantly believe in GOD. You got this, you can do it.

I am so thankful for

everything that GOD

has blessed me with

In order to live a better life, one must be thankful for their current situation. Be thankful for the life GOD has given you thus far. Being thankful changes your mood and brings you happiness. It keeps you positive. GOD blesses us with more when we are thankful and grateful. You can always want more for your life. However, don't focus on what you do not have or the aspects of your life that you are not happy about. Look at the glass as half full, not half empty. Next, shift your thoughts to how you can fill your glass to capacity.

Oprah Winfrey said, "Be thankful for what you have; you'll end up having more." If you concentrate on what you don't have, you will never have enough. The trick is to focus on what makes you happy and feel good about it. That will bring more blessings and happiness into your life. Just think, how does GOD want you to feel? Depressed, sad, down an out, fearful, happy, joyful, confident, or excited about life. Anytime your thoughts start to go down that dark negative tunnel, stop and say delete. Delete those negative thoughts and replace them with positive thoughts and ideas. Think about what you are thankful for, the people you are thankful for, and your experiences that you are thankful for. Think about the things in life that you are working on accomplishing and have the feeling and thought that you have already achieved those goals. Write down 5 things you are thankful for and 5 people you are thankful for. It's ok if you don't have 5 or more than 5. However, for those you do have call them and let them know why you appreciate them. Watch how blessings starts to flow your way from showing gratitude. Remember being thankful for where you are now and what you have now opens the gate for more blessings to be showered upon you.

I am destined for

GREATNESS.

Nothing is too hard for

me

Believe that you are destined for GREATNESS. Once you believe, everything else will fall right into place. This doesn't mean that you will not face any obstacles. Every obstacle we face makes us stronger and helps us gain more experience. When confronted with these obstacles remember that nothing is too hard for you. If you have a midterm or final exam coming up, believe that you will do well and pass it. Now you have to put in the work, study, go see the tutor (if necessary), and put in those extra hours. This might all seem daunting but it will be well worth it. The effort you put in will definitely pay off. Our perception of different obstacles we face is half the battle. Train your mind to think positively and have confidence in yourself. Believe in your intelligence. Remember, rough roads lead you to your success and happiness. GOD wants you to succeed and will never present you with anything that you can't handle. If it's an assignment at school, work, your business, or even life at home trust yourself and know that it is not too hard for you to complete any task. You have the skills and knowledge to do it. You are GREAT.

I finish everything I start successfully and in a timely manner

It's very imperative that you prioritize at this point in your life. You have to make the decision to start your assignments, projects, and homework in a timely manner to prevent cramming. When you wait until the last minute you don't give your best effort and you add unnecessary stress upon yourself. There are a few techniques that you can implement to prevent from cramming. Ultimately, this will help prioritize your time.

- *Get a planner or write in your notebook all of your*

assignments, exams, midterms, and projects dates.

- *Set a schedule for yourself. It's about balance and time management. You do not want to go from one extreme to the next, but you should enjoy your college years.*
- *Make deadlines for yourself. If you know you have a paper due in 2 weeks, make a deadline for your outline, research time, and rough copy. Knock out a little at a*

time so you don't feel overwhelmed.

- *Make time for the library. You will be surprised at how much work you get done when you are isolated. Being alone with your work makes it so much easier to stay on task.*
- *Finally make time for yourself. Do something you enjoy, relax, and let your hair down. Like I mentioned before, life is about balance and you need to enjoy your college*

experience along with getting your education.

Prioritizing your time will help you finish all your work in a timely manner, which will enhance the quality of your work. Believe in yourself and your skills. No assignment is too hard, as long as you give yourself enough time to thoroughly complete it. Give it your best and remember you got this, you are GREAT!

I Love to study and prepare for exam

The only way to feel confident when taking an exam is to be prepared for it. No one likes that nervous feeling before, during, and after an exam. That feeling of uncertainty, guessing on questions, and taking 10 minutes on a problem that should take less than 5 minutes can eat you up inside. Trust me, I've been there and it's not a good feeling. It's stressful. Exams are not hard when you properly prepare for them. This affirmation ties right into the previous one. Start studying and preparing early. You have a syllabus. Don't wait until the week of the exam or assignment to start studying for it. Review your notes daily. That information will get into your conscious and subconscious mind and you will learn it instead of just remembering it. You don't want to remember information just to pass an exam, you want to know it and gain more knowledge of that subject to prepare you for your future. Enjoy preparing and studying for your exams because everything you are learning now is bringing you closer to reaching your goals and living the life of your dreams. Know that you can pass every exam with flying colors. It all starts in your mind. When you prepare as if you know you will and have already passed your test, I promise you, you will get the grade that you deserve and want. There's a saying, Proper Preparation Prevents Poor Performance. You already know you have to prepare for your midterms and finals so you might as well enjoy the process. This will alleviate stress and help you enjoy your college experience rather than worrying about finals. Do something every day to prepare and love the preparation process. Once you pass your exams, celebrate yourself for your hard work. Remember our perception is everything, so tell yourself, "I love to study and prepare for exams because I know I am going to pass them." You are GREAT.

Every day and every

moment I am becoming

more and more disciplined

This is going to be one of your biggest challenges in college. No one is there to tell you to get up, no one to cook your food, no one to wash your clothes. It's all on you now, but the great thing is you can do it. Each time you make the decision to wake up early, study a little longer, or to not go to that party you are gaining more discipline. After college, having discipline is a must. You have to learn to say no when you really want to say yes.

Jesse Owens said, "We all have dreams, but in order to make dreams come into reality, it takes an awful lot of determination, self-discipline, and effort." A good strategy to use is to think about the end result that you desire. Think about why you are in college and the goals you want to accomplish in life. College is just a stage, a chapter, a part of your life, but this is where you start your foundation. Trust me, what you do now will affect your life later. Work hard on your discipline and continue to tell yourself you are disciplined. When you are disciplined you are more confident. When you are confident, you will be successful. Everyone wants to be successful in life but everyone is not disciplined enough to put in the work and time that success requires. Be a part of the disciplined crew. The crew that knows what they want out of life and is willing to put the work in every single day towards making their goals and dreams a reality. Remember you are GREAT.

I live my life with a purpose

Every single day counts. We cannot get back yesterday. Enjoy your life and live it with a purpose. I know you are young and you may not know what you want to do with your life right now or what career you want to pursue. However, you can still live your life with a purpose right now. Live to grow every day, to show integrity every day, to be happy every day. A great motivational speaker Eric Thomas asked the question, What's your why? He said, "once you know your why, your life will change." Why do you get up every day? Why do carry yourself a certain way? If you don't know your why, ask yourself that question every day when you wake up. Pray about it, look from within, and ask GOD for clarity. Know, trust, and believe that the answer will come to you. One good step to take if you don't know your why is to start your day by making a list of things you want to accomplish that day or week. Think about the type of impact you want to have on someone's life. Love yourself and know that your life has a purpose even if you are unsure of it right now. We are all born with our own individualized gifts and talents. We are all born for a reason. You will have a major impact on the world. Trust yourself and have confidence in yourself. I know every day may not be your best but that doesn't change who you are. You are born with Greatness inside of you. It's just a matter of time before the rest of the world sees and witness how GREAT you are.

It is always too early to

give up on my goals

Sometimes life can seem hard, stressful, and overwhelming. Especially when you have 4 finals, 2 papers, and a presentation due. Yes, that is a lot on your plate but you can handle it. One thing you can do to help yourself is prioritize your task and complete the longest or most difficult task first. Prioritizing will alleviate stress and help you produce a better quality of work. Another tool to use is keeping a positive mind state. Remember you can handle it. Graduating from college is a goal that you set after high school and you are going to feel amazing after accomplishing your goal. But graduating is only the beginning of your life.

What else do you want out of life? What are your goals and aspirations? How will you impact the world? Whatever your goals are know, trust, and believe you can do it. At times your vision may get blurry because you are facing adversity. Things may not go according to plan, or the results you want don't come as fast as you want. That doesn't mean you will not get to the finish line. Continue to work and never give up. Dr. Joseph Murphy told us to imagine the end and make it reality. Follow it through and you will get definite results. So, don't give in and keep pushing. Trust that GOD will bless you at the perfect time. See the end result and you will get there. A great exercise to help you to accomplish your goals is to write them down. Make plans and create the steps you need to take in order to reach your goals. Next, read them every day, every morning, every night, and whenever you can during the day. Put daily reminders in your phone so you will see your goals every day. You have to feed your conscious and subconscious mind with positivity about your future goals. Remember, it is always too early to give up on your goals. GOD will never give up on you. You can do it. Trust yourself, believe in yourself, and have faith in yourself because GOD does. GOD has blessed you and will continue to bless you with all the skills and abilities for you to live a prosperous life and accomplish your goal. Go do it because you are GREAT.

GOD has blessed me and

will continue to bless me

with the talents,

knowledge, and abilities to

change the world

positively

Yes, you have it already! Believe in yourself. Right now, you are perfecting your craft and all of your experiences are leading up to you to show the world how GREAT you are. GOD has blessed us all with individualized traits so that we can have a positive impact and influence on this world. It's up to us to practice, study, and work on our talents so that we can be the best version of ourselves. It takes time so be patient. Stay focused on always getting better and doing your best. Do not let past failures or past mistakes determine your future. Keep positivity on your mind and know that you are becoming and you are already the person you need to be. Now is the time to work hard so that later you can live the life you want. Put in those extra study hours, read those books others aren't reading, and keep practicing. While putting in the work, visualize your future. GOD has already mapped out the perfect life for you. You are GREAT and you will have a positive impact on this world!!!

I always do my best and

give 110%

Tell yourself this every day. It's going to be times when you just want to hurry up and finish that paper, quiz, or exam. But trust me, doing just enough is not showing your GREATNESS. The work you put in now will show. When you give 110% and do your best every day, on every assignment, and on every presentation, it becomes a part of your character. It becomes second nature to you. You will catch yourself whenever you give less than your best and you will learn to check yourself and make the proper corrections and adjustments. The

Greats in life put in the extra time and effort. There will be nights when you have to sacrifice, not go hang out, or not go to that party. Don't worry about it, you will have plenty of time to enjoy yourself and there will be more parties. Right now, you need to stay focused on the task at hand and doing your best. There is a powerful quote that says "Always do your best. What you plant now, you will harvest later." You are preparing for that job of your dreams, running your own business, or being that star athlete/entertainer. You can do it.

Everything you are doing now is setting you up for your bright and beautiful future. Remember you are GREAT. Don't think anything else.

I am learning from all of

my experiences

Every single day is filled with different experiences that we learn from. Of course, everything doesn't go the way we want, but we can learn from those experiences too. Your interactions with your friends, classmates, and professors are all learning opportunities. Learn how to deal with things that do not go your way. It's all about how you react to the situation. Stay positive during these times and understand that you are going through this to learn a lesson and you are becoming a better person and a better version of yourself. On the other hand, when you experience something great that makes you feel good cherish it. Hold on to those feelings and remember why you had those feelings. Therefore, in the future you can create those feelings again. Once you understand you can learn from all your experiences, you will become more optimistic and you will become a happier person. Everything happens for a reason. GOD will never put you in a situation that you cannot handle. Yes, class might seem hard and you might feel swamped during finals but remember you have the strength, knowledge, and abilities to work through this time in your life. This college experience is preparing you for your future. You are creating the future you want now. You are building the discipline you need to be successful after college. You are a creator. You are GREAT. Never let a bad experience get you down. Learn from it so you will be prepared if a similar experience comes across your life.

I am a great reader and I

understand everything

that I read

During this time in your life a lot of reading is required of you. Sometimes it can feel like you are reading words in different languages and big words that you don't understand or comprehend. Before you think it's too much or too hard for you, believe in your own personal knowledge and abilities. You are here for a reason and the classes you have are preparing you for your future. Everything happens in divine order and you can handle every single reading assignment and chapter that you read.

First, you want to make sure you give yourself enough time. Proper time management is very important. You don't want to speed read and cram at the last minute. Give yourself enough time to be able to go back and reread to make sure you are comprehending the concepts that are being covered.

Here are a few tips to help you when you feel like your plate is full. One good rule of thumb is to break down lengthy reading assignments into smaller sections. Next you should look for charts, pictures, and graphs. Pay close attention to notes and margins, italicized words, and bold-face words. These are the most important factors in that chapter or section. Another good tip is to rewrite your paragraph headings and turn them into questions. After reading each paragraph, answer the question to check for understanding. If you cannot clearly answer the question that is a sign that you need to reread that section. Finally, and this is something we've been doing for a while, highlight key points in your text. This will help you remember the most important facts. This improves your note taking and studying process as well. It is very important that you believe in yourself and your abilities at all times. Especially when your workload is heavy. Repeat this to yourself before you read, when you are tired of reading, and when you are finish reading, I am a great reader and I understand everything that I read. I am GREAT!!!

I believe in myself. I am

GREAT

You were born GREAT! GOD blessed you with the opportunity of life so you have GREATNESS within you. Merriam-Webster defines GREATNESS as being exceptionally high quality. That's who you are! You are exceptional. You are high quality. No matter what you have been through in your life, whatever failures you think you might've had, you are still GREAT. You have to remind yourself this every single day. When you think of yourself as GREAT, others will too. Your GREATNESS will show in the way you walk, the way you talk, and you will feel GREAT. Once you start to feel GREAT, GREAT things will happen to you and for you. GOD will send blessings your way that you have never imagined. The goal in life is to feel good about yourself no matter the situation. If you are not where you want to be, do not worry about your current situation. Think about and visualize where you want to be, where you are going to be, and where your goal destination is at. Then, think about the emotions you will feel once you get there. That is what being GREAT is all about. We all face obstacles in life, but we have to remain feeling GREAT throughout these obstacles. Susan Taylor said. "Whatever we believe about ourselves and our abilities comes true for us." Believe you are GREAT! Know you are GREAT! It will come to fruition. GOD has blessed you to be GREAT! Remind yourself of this every day.

I am strong-minded. I always make the right decision

Your mind is very powerful. Believe you are strong-minded and you can control your thoughts. Our thoughts come to life so keep your thoughts positive and on accomplishing your goals. Not every decision we make we might get the results we want at the time we want it. However, in those scenarios we must view it as a learning lesson. This doesn't mean you will not get the results you want, it just means it wasn't time for it yet. We learn from all of our experiences so do not beat yourself up and think you made the wrong decision. Trust yourself and remember GOD is always with you, every single moment of your life. Everything starts in our mind. Our thoughts create our future. So, practice controlling your thoughts. The better you are at controlling your thoughts, the stronger your mind is.

When you are strong-minded you are strong-willed. You are disciplined, and you do not worry or fear anything. When you are strong-minded you trust yourself and you trust GOD. When you are strong-minded you believe and know that you always make the right decisions.

Your assignment for this week is to record some major and minor decisions you've made. Write down how they made you feel and write down what you received from making those decisions. Did it set well with you? Did you learn something from it? Did it affect anybody else besides yourself? When you look at your reflections do not get down on yourself if you think you didn't make the right decisions. Rather think about how you would handle that situation if you had to make a similar decision in the future. Remember GOD is with you every single moment of your life and will always be with you. Remember you are GREAT and you are strong-minded.

I fear nothing. GOD is always with me

What is fear? Where did it come from? When was the first time you feared something? Why do we fear? Do we fear people, situations, work, responsibilities? The New Oxford American dictionary defines fear as an unpleasant emotion caused by the belief that someone or something is dangerous, likely to cause pain, or a threat. Another definition is a feeling of anxiety concerning the outcome of something or the safety and well-being of someone. Fear starts in our mind.

Let me ask you this, do you think GOD wants you to have fear in your heart? Do you think GOD wants you to be fearful? When we know, trust, and believe that GOD is with us and in us all of the time and never away from us, we will not fear anything. That is the first step to overcome any fear we have. GOD does not want us to be fearful. The next step in overcoming fear is to recognize and acknowledge why you are fearing something. Is it the fear of talking in front of a big crowd? Fear of rejection? Fear of failure? Try to understand what is holding you back and remind yourself you are GREAT. Remind yourself that GOD is with you and GOD doesn't want you to fear anything. Once you face that fear you will realize that nothing is too hard for you and you have the confidence to overcome any obstacle that you come across. Believing in yourself, believing that GOD is always with you, and seeing the outcome you desire is how we overcome our fears. Today remind yourself, I fear nothing because I believe in myself, I know GOD is always with me, and GOD believes in me!!!

I can accomplish all of

my goals and dreams

We all have dreams and goals we want to accomplish in life. During our lives' we have witnessed people that are living out their dreams and we have also witnessed people that have given up on their dreams. What is the difference in between those two different groups of people? It is favor? Being lucky? Being born into the right family? Let me tell you this, the answer to those questions doesn't matter. Do not ever compare your life to someone else's. We are all born with our own talents, gifts, and abilities we are to share with the world. It is up to you the individual, to put in the work, have discipline, and trust that GOD is always blessing you throughout your life. Trust, know, and believe that you can and will accomplish your goals and dreams. GOD will bless you with everything that you want and need during your life. This is what most people call faith. Have faith in yourself and in GOD. Have patience because you might not get there as fast as you want, but trust me you will get there having perseverance. A quote from Wilma Rudolph states, "Never underestimate the power of dreams and the human spirit. We are all the same notion: the potential for greatness lives within each of us." Tell yourself this and know that you have all that it takes to accomplish your goals and live the life of your dreams. Stay focused, do not ever give up, and visualize yourself living the life that you want. Remember you are GREAT!!!

I stay positive at all times

This is difficult for some people to do because as soon as something does not go the way they want, they get upset and let their negative thoughts take over. The goal in life is to have an optimistic view about all of your encounters. Now we know we you can't stay happy and upbeat 100 percent of the time, but the trick is to catch yourself when you start to feel down or depressed. Block those negative thoughts and feelings and replace them with positive thoughts. Optimism is hopefulness and confidence about the future or the successful outcome of something. Basically, if you are optimistic you are hopeful and confident about your future. That is the key to success. Don't worry about the present as much. If things aren't going your way then stay focused on your goals, continue to work towards your goals, and stay confident that you will reach your goals. Believe and know that you are successful and you will have a successful future. You have to KNOW! Don't have any doubt! Yes, you might face a few failures, roadblocks, and obstacles but that doesn't mean you will not meet success. Stay positive throughout those times because every obstacle we encounter increases our knowledge, builds resiliency, and improves our character. So, take on those battles with a smile, loving heart, and a positive mind. They are helping you to become the person you need to be. You are successful. Remind yourself this every day and all day. Stay positive and remember you are GREAT!!!

<u>GOD blessed me with all</u>

<u>that I need at the perfect</u>

<u>time and place in my life</u>

GOD has blessed you with GREATNESS! GOD has blessed you every single day of your life. GOD will never stop blessing you. Think back to a time when you thought you were in a bad stage of your life. Now look at where you are now. GOD blessed you throughout that situation and everything you have been through. GOD is always with us and is in you. So, you never have to worry about anything. The problem with most of us is, we want things to happen as soon as possible. We want it right now and don't want to wait. But trust

GOD's timing. GOD's timing is perfect. GOD blesses us with everything that we need and want when it is the perfect time for us. So, if you are feeling like you are not successful enough or not in the place you thought you would be by now, don't worry and trust GOD. Do not compare your life to someone else's. When we compare we bring unnecessary stress to ourselves. Instead of comparing, appreciate your life and be thankful for where you are headed. Have faith that GOD is working on your success story every single day. Remember what we think is what we create. So always think, know, and believe that GOD is blessing you with everything you want and need at the perfect time for YOU. It takes patience and faith and you have both. Patience will help you stay focused on the goal at hand. Faith will show how grateful and thankful you are for your life. Remember you are GREAT and if you start feeling down, stressed, or overwhelmed, tell yourself: GOD blesses me with everything that I need and want at the perfect time in my life!

The Wrap Up

The number one thing to remember after reading this book is that none of this information matters if you do not believe in yourself. Everything starts from within. Trust yourself, believe in yourself, and trust GOD. You are destined for greatness, believe in the process and never lose faith in yourself or in GOD. You are GREAT and will have a positive impact on this world!!!!